It's almost time for Andy and Woody to head out to Cowboy Camp. But before they go, Woody must rescue Bo Peep from the evil Dr. Pork Chop! Woody needs the help of Buzz Lightyear to save the fair Bo Peep from a vicious shark or death by monkeys.

You can help Woody, too. Find Buzz and these other toys that can assist in this daring rescue.

Buzz

Battle Bunny

Baby Commando

Chatterbox

Sergeant

Super Dude

Bongo Monkey

Woody was left behind from Cowboy Camp, but now he has a chance to be a real cowboy. Woody must save Wheezy from being sold at the yard sale. With the help of the family dog, Buster, Woody makes the trip into the yard. But where's Wheezy?

Look through all this old junk to help Woody find Wheezy. While you're at it, find Woody, Buster, and some other fun treasures.

Woody

Lava Lamp

Wheezy

Bicentennial Tea Pot

This Record Album

Roller Skates

Buster

BIKE 4 SALE

WOW

25¢

25¢

LITTLE TOYS

ROCK HOODLUM

Woody has been captured from the yard sale by Al from Al's Toy Barn! Now Woody is far from Andy's room and all his old friends. But it turns out that Woody was a big TV star and everyone from *Woody's Roundup* treats him like a star cowboy!

Look around Al's apartment to find this Woody merchandise.

Woody Button

Cowboy Woody Safety Scissors

Woody's Toothpaste

Woody's Fun Foam

Roundup Pencil Box

Cowboy Woody Soda

Woody's Roundup Thermos

A ndy's toys are on a mission to save Woody. They have to get to Al's Toy Barn, but first they must cross many lanes of the busiest traffic anyone has ever seen! It's risky business, but they're just the toys for the job!

As Buzz, Hamm, and Rex dodge traffic, look at all the crazy vehicles to find these fun things that seem a little too familiar.

Buzz Lightyear
Air Freshener

This Sign

This Cup Holder

This Dashboard
Ornament

HAMM

This License Plate

Funky Monkey
Fringe

There are so many toys and games inside Al's Toy Barn! Buzz, Rex, and Hamm have been searching for Woody among the shelves, but the only luck they've had has been finding a guidebook to defeating the evil Emperor Zurg for the Buzz Lightyear video game!

Look through the toys to find Buzz, Rex, Hamm, and these crazy characters they have met here.

Dirk Soldier

Rex

Buzz

Speedy Racer

Hamm

Rhonda Ragdoll

Evil Emperor Zurg

Al is taking Woody and the other Roundup collectibles to Japan to be put in a museum! Andy's toys need to rescue Woody from Al's suitcase before he gets loaded onto the plane. Some of the other Roundup toys help out because they don't want to go either.

You can help! Find Buzz, Woody, Jessie, Hamm, Rex, and Bullseye in this roller coaster ride of suitcases.

Buzz

Woody

Rex

Hamm

Bullseye

Jessie

Woody is back in Andy's room, and it's a celebration! Wheezy takes the microphone to serenade his toy friends.

Join the party and find these happy toys as they dance in delight.

Party Patty

Happy Hank

Joyful Jake

Good-Time Gil

Fun Fran

Silly Sally

Crazy Connie

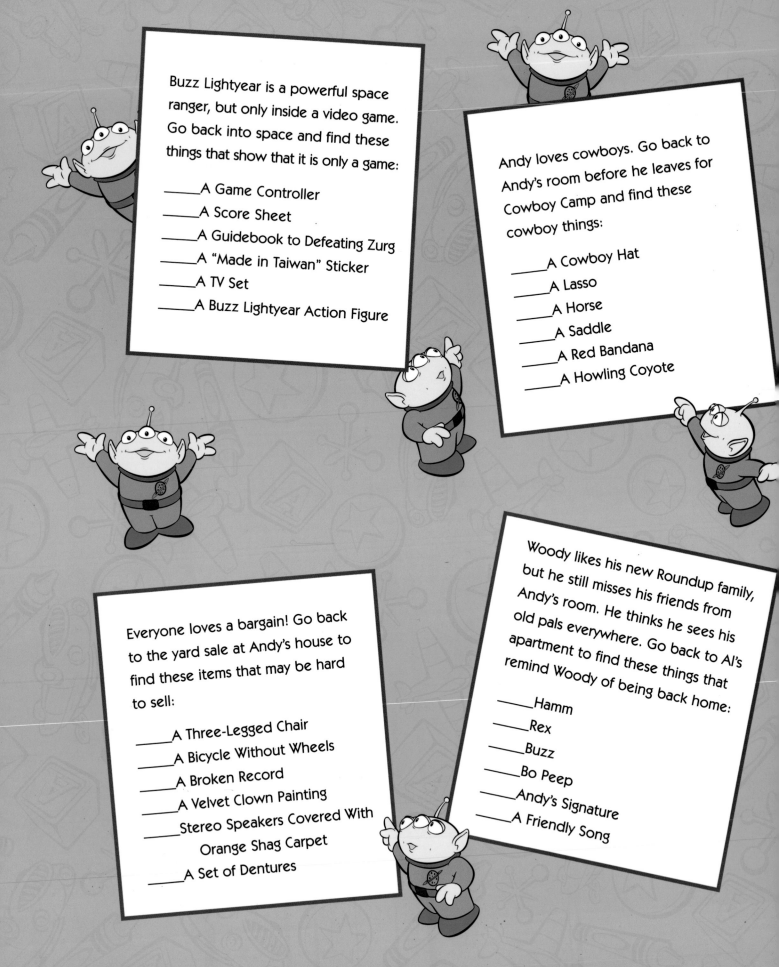

Buzz Lightyear is a powerful space ranger, but only inside a video game. Go back into space and find these things that show that it is only a game:

_____A Game Controller

_____A Score Sheet

_____A Guidebook to Defeating Zurg

_____A "Made in Taiwan" Sticker

_____A TV Set

_____A Buzz Lightyear Action Figure

Andy loves cowboys. Go back to Andy's room before he leaves for Cowboy Camp and find these cowboy things:

_____A Cowboy Hat

_____A Lasso

_____A Horse

_____A Saddle

_____A Red Bandana

_____A Howling Coyote

Everyone loves a bargain! Go back to the yard sale at Andy's house to find these items that may be hard to sell:

_____A Three-Legged Chair

_____A Bicycle Without Wheels

_____A Broken Record

_____A Velvet Clown Painting

_____Stereo Speakers Covered With Orange Shag Carpet

_____A Set of Dentures

Woody likes his new Roundup family, but he still misses his friends from Andy's room. He thinks he sees his old pals everywhere. Go back to Al's apartment to find these things that remind Woody of being back home:

_____Hamm

_____Rex

_____Buzz

_____Bo Peep

_____Andy's Signature

_____A Friendly Song